THE DANCE OF DEATH

THE DANCE OF DEATH

Les Simulachres & Historiées Faces de La Mort

designed by HANS HOLBEIN
and cut in wood by HANS LÜTZELBURGER

*Introductory essays by Philip Hofer
and Amy Turner Montague*

THE CYGNET PRESS
Privately Printed at The Godine Press · Boston · 1974

79106

Library of Congress Card Catalogue Number
74-81510
International Standard Book Number
0-87923-102-5

For Frances Hofer

ACKNOWLEDGEMENTS

A SET OF PROOFS have been graciously lent by Frances Hofer to make most of the reproductions in this book. This set is nearly complete, lacking only the cuts depicting the 'Consequences of the Fall' and the 'Astrologer' to make the forty-one found in the first edition. These two woodcuts have been reproduced from the first edition (1538), *Les Simulacres & Historiées Faces de La Mort*. The 'Beggar' first appeared, surrounded by type, in the 1545 *Imagines Mortis*, from which we have made our reproduction. In 1547 that cut appeared in sequence with the others, with Bible verse and quatrain. Eleven additional cuts also appeared in editions of that year. Our reproductions of the 'Beggar' as it appeared in sequence, and of nine of the eleven new subjects are from the 1547 *Les Images de La Mort*. The 'Drunkard' and the 'Fool' have been taken from the 1549 *Simolachri, Historie, e Figure de La Morte* which has better impressions of the woodcuts. In 1562 the last five new subjects were added, and these have been reproduced from the *Les Images de La Mort* of that date. Only a few copies of this edition contain the two woodcuts of the young couple. Each of the above mentioned books is at the Houghton Library of Harvard University. We have printed our reproductions in order of historical appearance.

The Bible verses and French quatrains which we have printed opposite the reproductions accompanied the woodcuts as they appeared in books. The first forty-one texts were taken from the first edition. The next twelve texts are from the 1547 *Les Images de La Mort*, and the remaining five from the 1562 edition of the same title. A few simple changes were made in orthography, with the intention of rendering the texts more readable. We have adopted the modern usage of j's, v's and u's. Where the original text included contractions, we have spelled out the words. The King James Version has been used for the translation of the Bible verses. In a few instances, indicated with asterisks, we have departed from the King James where it did not convey the meaning of the Vulgate verses.

We wish to thank David Godine, Eleanor Sayre, Eleanor McLaughlin, R. Lynwood Montague, and Lance Hidy for their support and advice. Special thanks are due to Eleanor Garvey for her continual assistance and encouragement.

PHILIP HOFER
KATHARINE HOMANS
AMY MONTAGUE

INTRODUCTORY ESSAYS

Holbein's *Dance of Death* Woodcuts

HANS HOLBEIN the Younger, (1497-1543), was surely one of the most important and creative artists of his day. Born at Augsburg, in Germany, he moved at the age of eighteen to Basle, Switzerland, where he was active from 1515 to 1528. From 1532 until he died, he lived and worked mainly in England, where he became far and away the principal artist at the court of Henry VIII.

Not only was Holbein a supreme portraitist, but his religious paintings – especially in his earlier years – his murals, mythological subjects, designs for heraldic shields, emblems, and stained glass, are equally fine – only less well known. Nor did he feel it beneath his dignity, at any period in his life, to design exquisite drawings for goldsmiths and silversmiths, as well as title pages, historiated borders, printers' marks, and initials for prominent publishers and printers. He also became quite widely renowned for two print series, both of which appeared in book form. The larger of

these consists of eighty-six small (6.5 x 8 cm.) woodcuts to illustrate the Old Testament in the Bible. The
other major print set contains fifty-eight even more
imaginative and powerful – although smaller (6.5 x
5 cm.) – Dance of Death scenes which are the subject
of this publication.

Hardly any woodcuts ever made were so influen-
tial on contemporary and later artists; for they were
copied, or imitated, scores of times ever since 1526
when the first forty-one of them seem to have been
finished. Holbein did not usually cut his woodblocks
himself, but he drew on them. His most gifted
woodcutter was Hans Lützelburger, also from Augsburg, whose technical genius matched Holbein's style
perfectly. All Holbein's woodcuts are on a fairly
small scale. But they are monumental in concept.

After Lützelburger died in 1526, unknown wood-
cutters chiefly served Holbein well, although with
varying skill. The English artisans were the poorest.
Since none of the *Dance of Death* woodcuts are signed
by Holbein, and no signed drawing is known for any
other of his woodcuts, the question arises how we
can be sure Holbein designed the *Dance of Death*
woodcuts at all! Contemporary texts mention him
as a master in this area; some other of his woodcuts

are signed, as well as borders–usually with his initials 'HH'. The final decision must be made on the basis of style, power, and imaginative content. On this basis there is little doubt, although mystery still surrounds their creation: 'when' and 'for what purpose'? It is easy to say 'who else could have designed them', and that they were meant for illustration, but it is impossible to prove, despite over a century of scholarly research and avid discussion. Analogies can, of course, be found with his work in other media. Actually, the cuts were generally accepted as by Holbein during the first fifty years–and decidedly before 1600.

For twelve years the *Dance of Death* woodblocks, except for the striking off of a limited number of 'proofs' with either italic or gothic (fraktur) letter captions in German, seem to have remained unused. Woltmann, an excellent early authority, believed that the proofs with italic printed captions are the earlier. Still, broken lines are to be found in both varieties of 'proofs'. Complete sets of forty-one, in varying states of preservation, are to be found at the British Museum, London, the Berlin Print Cabinet, the Bibliothèque Nationale in Paris, the Museum at Basle, and the print collection at Karlsruhe, Germany.

In the United States, the Metropolitan Museum,

New York, purchased a complete set in the early 1920's, and the writer of this essay bought the first 'von Lanna' (privately owned) set for the Fogg Museum at Harvard in 1928. Subsequently, he was able to secure the second, incomplete 'von Lanna' series (thirty-six out of forty-one proofs) personally at the Henry Oppenheimer Sale in London in 1936, and has since been able nearly to complete it by adding three more. As this set is generally superior to both the Fogg and Metropolitan complete runs – also nearly all of them have their captions – the reproductions in this publication have been made from them.

The *Dance of Death* woodcuts finally appeared publicly at Lyons, in France, in small quarto book form (as here) under the French title *Les Simulachres & Historiées Faces de La Mort*. The printers were the brothers Gaspar and Melchior Trechsel working for the publishers Frellon. They only put one cut on each page, with Biblical quotations in Latin above, and French quatrains beneath, the authorship of which is still disputed. Some authorities believe the writer to be Jean de Vauzelles, the author of the dedication. Others suggest as the writer Gilles Corrozet, to whom the text accompanying the Old Testament woodcuts is attributed, since this larger print series was produced in the same year by the same printers and publishers.

After 1538, there were a number of further editions, and issues–notably those of 1542, 1543, 1545, 1547, 1554 and 1562–in French, Italian, and Latin, mainly put out by the Frellons. In 1543, a cut portraying a crippled beggar was added, making forty-two in all. In 1545, eleven more new subjects were introduced for a total of fifty-three. Finally, in 1562, five more woodcuts appeared of which two seem possibly by another hand than Holbein's – a French artist? Yet they reflect a good deal of Holbein's style and grace. A young man and young woman are featured in these, who are referred to, by the quatrains, as a married couple. In addition to being very beautifully cut, with perhaps an especially French flavor, they are the scarcest of all the series. For they appear only in this edition, and not in every copy, since the leaves on which they are placed repeat the signature marks C6 and C7. No proofs of these woodcuts are recorded.

Did Holbein intend the four woodcuts of children first to be seen in 1545 (two years after the artist's death at London in 1543) for the *Dance of Death* series? It can be doubted; they are very different in spirit and subject matter, although the quatrains endeavor to tie them in. All the children seem so happy with their military or Bacchic trophies, and no skeleton appears. Here is just another mystery surrounding the books and the cuts which scholarship so far has been unable to resolve.

Hans Lützelburger's monogram, 'HL', is contained in one of the original forty-one woodcuts believed to have been finished by 1526 in proof form. It can be seen in a cartouche on the left, at the foot of 'Die Hertzoginn's' (the 'Duchess') bed. Further evidence of Lützelburger's coöperation with Holbein is furnished by a proof sheet of Holbein's Dance of Death historiated initials which is fully signed by him in a legend: 'HAnns Lützelburger formschneider, genannt Franck', belonging to the British Museum.

Now one should come to a discussion of the individual subjects and artistic qualities of this *Dance of Death* as a whole, totalling altogether fifty-eight illustrations. It begins with four subjects directly derived from the Book of Genesis: 'God creating Eve', 'the Temptation', 'the Expulsion from the Garden of Eden', and 'Adam' (it is assumed) working the soil, while 'Eve' nurses a baby, holding her spinning rod – all obligations they were, then, forced to assume. If these prints were not exactly the same dimensions as the woodcuts which follow, one would hardly expect them, any more than the happy children, although a skeleton–'Death'–does appear in the last two of the first four. It is the fifth cut which brings one up with a start: the 'Gebeyn aller Menschen' (mankind reduced to skeletons). Then the true Dance of Death is at once introduced! Like a title page to the series, it proposes that all will be brought to account, as they are in the prints which follow. At first they appear in hierarchical order: 'Pope', 'Emperor', 'King', 'Cardinal', 'Empress', 'Queen', 'Bishop', etc.

Some critics have observed that the 'King' resembles Francis I, at this time King of France. But there is no consistency in depicting known people. The 'Emperor' probably is not Charles V, Francis' contemporary. Nor is there any marked analogy in the way each personage faces 'Death'. Some seem positively tranquil ('King', 'Empress'); others are filled with terror ('Queen', 'Monk'); some resist ('Nobleman', 'Knight'); others follow 'Death' ('Pastor', 'Old Man'). The 'Doctor' is, characteristically perhaps, only mildly surprised; the 'Miser' is frantic as 'Death' gathers his money into a large tray directly before his eyes!

The backgrounds vary enormously – from small intimate scenes within a room ('Duchess', 'Countess') to wide landscapes ('Farmer'), which can be magnified many times and still retain a far reaching vista, distant hills, and brilliant sunset. There is occasionally an almost complete lack of background, as in one of the later scenes where a horse and cart filled with barrels has fallen to the ground. Here 'Death' takes a very active part – actually breaking the cart into pieces.

It is to be hoped that the reader will permit some personal prejudice, and allow for differences in taste in the artistic criticism that follows. To the writer, familiar over many years with Holbein's cuts, and other 'Death' series such as the *Danse Macabre* of Guy Marchant, Paris, 1486, and Robert Gobin's *Les Loups Ravissans*, Paris, circa 1503, this later Holbein print series is the most perfectly balanced between realism and imagination, resignation and fear. It has the widest range of subjects. There are scenes of the utmost poignancy, as in the 'Child', where the contrast of expression in all the figures is at great variance, yet utterly convincing. And there are scenes of great natural beauty – the 'Farmer' plowing his field at sunset, or the elegant 'Countess' about to try on a lovely new dress. . . .

Except for the curious anomaly of the four representations of children, without 'Death', the later cuts are as powerful as the early ones, and as well conceived. Technically, one can believe Lützelburger may have cut the print of the 'Robber' who assaults a woman peasant with her market basket still poised on her head. The agony of the crippled 'Beggar' could not be better portrayed, seated as he is, in abject misery, while onlookers escape, or only stare curiously at a considerable distance. To the writer's Edwardian–if not Victorian!–eyes, the 'Drunkard', who is throwing up at the dinner table, is fairly repulsive, and so is the 'Mad Man' (or 'Fool'?). But one must remember the freer popular attitude of the sixteenth century on these subjects. At any period, the 'Blind Man' would be considered superb. Holbein portrays him in a landscape that equals nearly anything in German art.

Critics have, however, rightly remarked a strong Italian influence in Holbein's graphic production. Basle is situated in the center of Europe–at the crossroads of northern and southern styles. Holbein shows the cross-fertilization of several cultures better than anyone of his time. More delicate in his perceptions than Albrecht Dürer, Holbein is also less complicated in his compositions, and in the paraphernalia he brings into play. It is not his realism alone that gives Holbein a wider appeal than his great German contemporary to people of other countries, but the combination of his many and varied talents, his sensibility. At his best, Holbein transcends the usually more powerful, and intellectual, Dürer in his scenes of grace and beauty.

Of all the Dance of Death series, Holbein's is the one by which the others must be measured. It is, truly, the definitive one, as is indicated by its greater and continuing influence over four centuries. Finally, it is the most subtle. While it is the smallest in scale, it is the greatest in total effect.

PHILIP HOFER
Cambridge, Massachusetts
January 1974

A Short History of the
Dance of Death

THE DANCE OF DEATH theme is a product
of the late Middle Ages. Defined simply, it rep-
resents living men of various social stations encount-
ering either the dead or death personified. Originat-
ing in France, the Dance was later portrayed in Germany, England, Switzerland, Austria, Italy and Spain.
Representations were created in a variety of media:
drama, painting, poetry, sculpture, woodcut, stained
glass, tapestry, manuscript and printed book. This essay is a brief description of the Dance of Death's
place in the popular piety of its time. I hope to give
our modern reader an idea of the response of the sixteenth century reader to Holbein's book.

The earliest recorded instance of the Dance of
Death theme is in dramatic form. According to a
document found in the archives of a church in Caud-
ebec, Normandy, a drama was performed there in
1393. The document has been lost, but the abbot
Miette derived the following from it: 'The actors

represented all levels of society, from the sceptre to the shepherd's crook. One by one they departed, to show that each man comes to his end, the king in the same manner as the shepherd. This dance. . . is none other than the famous *danse macabre*.'[1]

Only two other dramatic representations are known. One is recorded in the accounts of the Dukes of Burgundy: 'To Nicaise de Cambray, painter, living in the town of Douai, to help him to defray his expenses in the month of September of the year 1449, in the town of Bruges, where he acted before the aforesaid lord, in his mansion, with his other companions, a certain play, history and morality relating to the fact of the *Danse macabre*, 8 francs.'[2] In 1453 the third recorded drama was performed at Besançon. It is mentioned in an account book written in Latin: 'That the seneschal has to pay to Jean de Calais sacrist of St. Jean, for four gallons of wine, furnished by the said sacrist to those who on the tenth of July last, after the hour of mass, performed the Dance of Death (*Chorea Machabaeorum*) in the church of St. John the Evangelist, on the occasion of

1. Emile Mâle, *L'Art Religieux de la Fin du Moyen Age en France* (Paris, 1925), p. 361.
2. James M. Clark, *The Dance of Death in the Middle Ages and the Renaissance* (Glasgow, 1950), p. 92.

the Provincial Chapter of the Friars Minor.'[3]

The first known pictorial representation of the Dance was painted during the years 1424 and 1425 at the cemetery of the Church of the Holy Innocents in Paris. In the *Journal d'un Bourgeois de Paris* the anonymous author recorded: 'It is in the year 1425 also that the *danse macabre* was completed at the Innocents; it was begun in the month of August 1424 and was finished the following Lent.'[4] The mural was done on the southern wall of the cemetery. Inside the wall was a cloister; above the cloister, charnel houses were built. The cemetery doubled as a marketplace, and the cloister and charnel houses were frequented by Parisians *en promenade*. In such a location, the mural was a familiar sight to the people of Paris.

The mural was destroyed in the seventeenth century, but fortunately there are indications of its nature. In the Bibliothèque Nationale there are two manuscript copies of the verses which accompanied it. And, in 1485, the Paris printer Guyot Marchant published the *Danse Macabre*, the first known book

3. Clark, *The Dance of Death in the Middle Ages and the Renaissance*, p. 92.

4. *Journal d'un Bourgeois de Paris* (Paris, 1963), p. 90.

to contain a representation of the Dance of Death. The artist and cutter of the illustrations are unknown, and the book itself does not claim to be a copy of the painting at the Innocents. But the verses in the book correspond to those in the manuscripts at the Bibliothèque and are therefore the same as those painted at the Innocents. The woodcuts, in all but a few minor instances, conform perfectly to the text, so it is likely that they are renditions of the scenes on the cemetery wall. For the purpose of making the Dance suitable to book form, Marchant presented only four figures on each page; however, to imagine the mural at the Innocents, one must picture a continuous procession. On the following page is a reproduction of the cut from Marchant's book showing the physician and the lover, each with his *mort*.

The Dance of Death at the Innocents was a didactic work, with a message common not only to other Dance representations but also to contemporary devotional practices and to preaching. The poet of the Innocents exhorted his reader to recognize that no man, whatever his place in society, can escape the Dance. The reader is then admonished to do good deeds, and to go to confession and mass. These are the final verses: 'O mortal man and reasonable be-

ing! If, after death, you do not wish to be damned
you must, at least once a day, think of your loath-
some end so that you may have a long life and die
well.'[5]

The frequent meditation on death and physical
decay was not a superficial exercise resulting in a happy end. Rather, it was one portion of late medieval
devotional practice intended to help men in their
daily lives to place in the larger context of eternity
the things which concerned them. The exhortation
of the Dance at the Innocents is expressed more
thoughtfully by Thomas à Kempis in *The Imitation of
Christ*. This manual of private devotion, which at-
tained such great popularity in the late Middle Ages,
was written just prior to the painting of the mural at
the Innocents. Thomas exhorts his readers to medi-
tate on death in order to become repentant and do
good: 'Dear soul, from what peril and fear you
could free yourself, if you lived in holy fear, mind-
ful of your death. Apply yourself so to live now,
that at the hour of death, you may be glad and una-
fraid. Learn how to die to the world, that you may
learn to live with Christ. Learn now to despise all

5. Edward F. Chaney, *La Danse Macabré des Charniers des Saints
Innocents à Paris* (Manchester, 1945), p. 65.

earthly things, that you may go freely to Christ. Discipline your body now with penance, that you may enjoy a sure hope of salvation.'[6]

This meditation on death is similar to certain devotional practices associated with Christ's Passion. The relationship between the Dance and the Passion is actual: Crucifixion representations are found in the center of the Dance of Death paintings at both Kleinbasel and Berne. The Passion was a particularly popular object of devotion in the late Middle Ages. A special mass and certain prayers were dedicated to the five wounds of Christ and many visions and religious experiences were inspired by the Passion. Margery Kempe, a fifteenth century Englishwoman, followed her contemplation of a pietà with these words to a priest: 'Christ's death is as fresh to me as if he had died this same day, and so methinketh, it ought to be to you and to all Christian people.'[7] In both the Crucifixion and death meditations, a man would imagine vividly the moment of death, either Christ's or his own, as if it were in the present, in order to move himself to repentance.

The poem at the Innocents refers to death as a fre-

6. Thomas à Kempis, *The Imitation of Christ* (Baltimore, 1968), p. 59.
7. Margaret Aston, *The Fifteenth Century: The Prospect of Europe* (London, 1968), p. 200.

quent sermon topic of mendicant friars. 'You have often preached about death,' says Death to the friar, 'so you should marvel the less.'[8] The mural was itself the scene of eight days of intense preaching by a friar named Richard in 1429, as recorded by the author of the *Journal d'un Bourgeois de Paris*. The subject of these sermons 'at the place of the Dance of Death' is unknown. However, other sermons of Richard's are known to have been apocalyptic, moving the hearers to build bonfires of fine clothes, gaming tables and playing cards.

One fascinating aspect of the Dance of Death is the portrayal, in a rigidly hierarchical society, of death as the leveller of all distinctions among men. Contemporary preaching, in its emphasis on repentance, did not neglect this particular characteristic of death. For example, John Mirk, an Englishman, wrote a sermon in which he pointed out the uselessness of wealth for a dead man:

> For sum tyme, os Iohn Belete sayth, the comyn pepul weron byryed at home in here owne houce; but than was ther so grete stynch of the cors and so vyolent, that it mythe not ben suffred. Than, be comyn assent, they makyt a place otwyth

8. Chaney, *La Danse Macabré des Charniers des Saints Innocents à Paris*, p. 61.

the toun, and byried there the corses; but the ryche men thei weron byried on hullus and in roches vndur hullus, but thus was no sokur don to ham aftur hur deth. Wherefore ofton soules apperuth to hure frendys pleynyng sore that thei haddon none helpe. Wherefore holy chyrch is halowod be holy byschoppes, the wyche leton maken chyrch-yordys, and halowod hem, and makud to bryngon all to holy chyrch, so that alle schuldon haue parte of the suffrages of the masse and of holy chyrch.[9]

A passage from Dr. John Bromyard, Chancellor at Cambridge University about 1383, is worth mentioning: 'If we could but consider well how quickly we shall be placed beneath the feet not only of men, friend and foe alike, but of dogs, and the beasts of the field–where he who now rears and possesses mighty places shall have a hall whose roof touches his nose . . .–we should find little reason for pride. . . . *Sic transit gloria mundi!'*[10] Bromyard's words include the two aspects of the Dance of Death message that have been mentioned here: the levelling characteristic of death and the contemplation on death as a means to a better life.

The arts and the sermon had long been traditional

9. John Mirk, *Mirk's Festial* (London, 1905), p. 296.
10. G. R. Owst, *Preaching in Medieval England* (Cambridge, 1926), p. 343.

sources of lay piety. In the fifteenth century another source emerged: the printed book. The popularity of the Dance in book form was great; one year after Marchant's first printing, he reprinted the book and published a second similar work, the *Danse Macabre des Femmes*.

The most famous representation of the Dance of Death is, without doubt, Holbein's series of woodcuts, first published in 1538. It is justifiably renowned, not only for the beauty and ingenuity of Holbein's drawing, but also for the artistry of Lützelburger's cutting. In this book, the Dance of Death theme is beautifully adapted to book form. While Marchant simply broke into page-sized segments the continuous procession shown in the mural at the Innocents, Holbein abandoned the idea of procession. The reader of a book can study only one page at a time, and each of Holbein's pages contains a single detailed scene which stands meaningfully alone.

The texts in the two books also vary. Holbein's cuts are accompanied, not by the dialogue poem, but by Latin Scripture quotations and their French versifications. In some later editions the quotations appear in the vernacular.

Holbein's book, although very different from

Marchant's, stands in the tradition of the fifteenth century Dances. The levelling characteristic of death is depicted not only by the woodcuts but also by the Scripture passages, many of which are warnings to the wealthy. The devotional aspect of the earlier Dance of Death representations is present in this sixteenth century book; the woodcut series is preceded and followed by a number of essays on death and on righteous living as the way to prepare for it. The cuts, as well as the text, were meant to lead the reader to a virtuous life so that he might die well. To that end, the author of one of the essays petitions God: 'God grant grace to us all so well to think on all these aspects of Death, and so intently to admire them, that when by the will of God Death shall come to take us, assured by Him who has triumphed over it, we also shall be able to triumph, that through the merit of that triumphant Chariot of the Cross we may be able to arrive at that life where Death no more has power or force. Amen.'[11]

AMY TURNER MONTAGUE
Boston, Massachusetts
January 1974

11. *Les Simulachres & Historiées Faces de la Mort,* ed. and trans. Henry Green (London, 1869), p. 156.

REPRODUCTIONS

Les ſimulachres &

HISTORIEES FACES

DE LA MORT, AVTANT ELE

gammēt pourtraictes, que artifi
ciellement imaginées.

Vſus me   Genuit.

A LYON,

Soubz l'eſcu de COLOIGNE.

M. D. XXXVIII.

Formavit DOMINUS DEUS hominem de limo terræ,
ad imaginem suam creavit illum, masculum &
fœminam creavit eos.

GENESIS I & II

And the Lord God formed man of the dust of the ground,
. . . created man in his own image, . . . male and female
created he them. Genesis 2:7, 1:27

DIEU, Ciel, Mer, Terre, procrea
De rien demonstrant sa puissance
Et puis de la terre crea
L'homme, & la femme a sa semblance.

Die schöpffung aller ding.

Quia audisti vocem uxoris tuæ, & comedisti de
ligno ex quo preceperam tibi ne comederes &c.
GENESIS III

Because thou hast hearkened unto the voice of thy wife,
and hast eaten of the tree, of which I commanded thee,
saying, Thou shalt not eat of it &c. Genesis 3:17

ADAM fut par EVE deceu
Et contre DIEU mangea la pomme,
Dont tous deux ont la Mort receu,
Et depuis fut mortel tout homme.

Emisit eum DOMINUS DEUS de Paradiso voluptatis,
ut operaretur terram de qua sumptus eſt.
GENESIS III

*Therefore the Lord God sent him forth from the garden of
Eden, to till the ground from whence he was taken.
Genesis 3:23*

DIEU chassa l'homme de plaisir
Pour vivre au labeur de ses mains:
Alors la Mort le vint saisir,
Et consequemment tous humains.

Maledicta terra in opere tuo, in laboribus comedes
cunctis diebus vitæ tuæ, donec revertaris &c.
GENESIS III

Cursed is the ground in thy work; in sorrow shalt thou eat
of it all the days of thy life . . . till thou return &c.
Genesis 3:17,19 *

Mauldicte en ton labeur la terre.
En labeur ta vie useras,
Jusques que la Mort te soubterre.
Toy pouldre en pouldre tourneras.

Væ væ væ habitantibus in terra.
APOCALYPSIS VIII
Cuncta in quibus spiraculum vitæ est, mortua sunt.
GENESIS VII

Woe, woe, woe, to the inhabiters of the earth.   Rev. 8:13
All in whose nostrils was the breath of life . . . died.
Genesis 7:22

Malheureux qui vivez au monde
Tousjours remplis d'adversitez,
Pour quelque bien qui vous abonde,
Serez tous de Mort visitez.

Gebeyn aller menschen.

Moriatur sacerdos magnus.
IOSUE XX
Et episcopatum eius accipiat alter.
PSALMISTA CVIII

*Let the high priest die. Joshua 20:6 ***
And let another take his office. Psalm 109:8

Qui te cuydes immortel eſtre
Par Mort seras toſt depesché,
Et combien que tu soys grand prebſtre,
Ung aultre aura ton Evesché.

Der Bapſt.

Dispone domui tuæ, morieris enim tu, & non vives.
ISAIÆ XXXVIII
Ibi morieris, & ibi erit currus gloriæ tuæ.
ISAIÆ XXII

*Set thine house in order: for thou shalt die, and not live.
Isaiah 38:1
There shalt thou die, and there the chariots of thy glory
shall be. Isaiah 22:18*

De ta maison disposeras
Comme de ton bien transitoire,
Car là ou mort reposeras,
Seront les chariotz de ta gloire.

Der Keyser.

Sicut & rex hodie est, & cras morietur, nemo enim ex regibus aliud habuit.

ECCLESIASTICI X

And he that is to day a king to morrow shall die. *Sirach* (*Ecclesiasticus*) *10:10*

Ainsi qu'aujourdhuy il est Roy,
Demain sera en tombe close.
Car Roy aulcun de son arroy
N'a sceu emporter aultre chose.

Væ qui iustificatis impium pro muneribus, &
iustitiam iusti aufertis ab eo.

ESAIE V

*Woe unto them . . . which justify the wicked for reward,
and take away the righteousness of the righteous from
him! Isaiah 5:23*

Mal pour vous qui justifiez
L'inhumain, & plain de malice,
Et par dons le sanctifiez,
Ostant au juste sa justice.

Der Cardinal.

Gradientes in superbia potest Deus humiliare.

DANIE. IIII

Those that walk in pride he is able to abase. Daniel 4:37

Qui marchez en pompe superbe
La Mort ung jour vous pliera.
Comme soubz voz piedz ployez l'herbe,
Ainsi vous humiliera.

Die Keyſerinn.

Mulieres opulentæ surgite, & audite vocem meam.
Poſt dies, & annum, & vos conturbemini.

ISAIÆ XXXII

Rise up, ye women that are at ease; hear my voice . . . .
Many days and years shall ye be troubled. Isa. 32:9,10

Levez vous dames opulentes.
Ouyez la voix des trespassez.
Apres maintz ans & jours passez,
Serez troublées & doulentes.

Die Küniginn.

Percutiam paſtorem, & dispergentur oves.

XXVI MAR. XIIII

I will smite the shepherd, and the sheep shall be scattered.
Mark 14:27

Le paſteur aussi frapperay
Mitres & crosses renversées.
Et lors quand je l'attrapperay,
Seront ses brebis dispersées.

Der Bischoff.

Princeps induetur mœrore. Et quiescere faciam su⁄
perbiam potentium.

EZECHIE. VII

The prince shall be clothed with desolation. I will also
make the pomp of the strong to cease. Ezekiel 7:27,24

Vien, prince, avec moy, & delaisse
Honneurs mondains toſt finissantz.
Seule suis qui, certes, abaisse
L'orgueil & pompe des puissantz.

Der Hertzog.

Ipse morietur. Quia non habuit disciplinam, & in
multitudine ſtultitiæ suæ decipietur.

PROVER. V

*He shall die without instruction; and in the greatness of his
folly he shall go astray. Proverbs 5:23*

Il mourra, Car il n'a receu
En soy aulcune discipline,
Et au nombre sera deceu
De folie qui le domine.

Der Apt.

Laudavi magis mortuos quam viventes.

ECCLE. IIII

Wherefore I praised the dead which are already dead more than the living which are yet alive. Ecclesiastes 4:2

J'ay tousjours les mortz plus loué
Que les vifz, esquelz mal abonde,
Toutesfoys la Mort ma noué
Au ranc de ceulx qui sont au monde.

Quis est homo qui vivet, & non videbit mortem,
eruet animam suam de manu inferi?

PSAL. LXXXVIII

*What man is he that liveth, and shall not see death? shall
he deliver his soul from the hand of the grave? Ps.89:48*

Qui est celluy, tant soit grand homme,
Qui puisse vivre sans mourir?
Et de la Mort, qui tout assome,
Puisse son Ame recourir?

Der Edelman

Ecce appropinquat hora.
MAT. XXVI

Behold, the hour is at hand. Matthew 26:45

Tu vas au choeur dire tes heures
Priant Dieu pour toy, & ton proche.
Mais il fault ores que tu meures.
Voy tu pas l'heure qui approche ?

Der Thumherr.

Disperdam iudicem de medio eius.

AMOS II

I will cut off the judge from the midst thereof. Amos 2:3

Du mylieu d'eulx vous osteray
Juges corrumpus par presentz.
Point ne serez de Mort exemptz.
Car ailleurs vous transporteray.

Der Richter.

Callidus vidit malum, & abscondit se innocens, per-
transiit, & afflictus est damno.

PROVER. XXII

*A prudent man forseeth the evil, and hideth himself: but
the simple pass on, and are punished. Proverbs 22:3*

L'homme cault a veu la malice
Pour l'innocent faire obliger,
Et puis par voye de justice
Est venu le pauvre affliger.

Der Fürſprach.

Qui obturat aurem suam ad clamorem pauperis, &
ipse clamabit, & non exaudietur.

PROVER. XXI

*Whoso stoppeth his ears at the cry of the poor, he also shall
cry himself, but shall not be heard. Proverbs 21:13*

Les riches conseillez tousjours,
Et aux pauvres clouez l'oreille.
Vous crierez aux derniers jours,
Mais Dieu vous sera la pareille.

Der Ratßherr.

Væ qui dicitis malum bonum, & bonum malum,
ponentes tenebras lucem, & lucem tenebras, ponentes amarum dulce, & dulce in amarum.

ISAIÆ XV

Woe unto them that call evil good, and good evil; that put
darkness for light, and light for darkness; that put bit-
ter for sweet, and sweet for bitter! Isaiah 5:20

Mal pour vous qui ainsi osez
Le mal pour le bien nous blasmer,
Et le bien pour mal exposez,
Mettant avec le doulx l'amer.

Der Predicant.

Sum quidem & ego mortalis homo.

SAP. VII

I myself also am a mortal man, like to all.   Wisdom of
    Solomon 7:1

Je porte le sainct sacrement
Cuidant le mourant secourir,
Qui mortel suis pareillement.
Et comme luy me fault mourir.

Der Pfarrherr.

Sedentes in tenebris, & in umbra mortis, vinctos in
  mendicitate.

PSAL. CVI

*Such as sit in darkness and in the shadow of death, being
  bound in beggary. Psalm 107:10 ***

Toy qui n'as soucy, ny remord
Sinon de ta mendicité,
Tu sierras a l'umbre de Mort
Pour t'ouster de necessité.

Der Münch.

Est via quæ videtur homini iusta: novissima autem
eius deducunt hominem ad mortem.

PROVER. IIII

*There is a way which seemeth right unto a man, but the
end thereof are the ways of death. Proverbs 14:12*

Telle voye aux humains est bonne,
Et a l'homme tresjuste semble.
Mais la fin d'elle a l'homme donne,
La Mort, qui tous pecheurs assemble.

Die Nunne.

Melior est mors quam vita.

ECCLE. XXX

Death is better than life. Sirach (Ecclesiasticus) 30:17*

En peine ay vescu longuement
Tant que nay plus de vivre envie,
Mais bien je croy certainement,
Meilleure la Mort que la vie.

Medice, cura teipsum.
LUCÆ IIII

Physician, heal thyself. Luke 4:23

Tu congnoys bien la maladie
Pour le patient secourir,
Et si ne scais teſte eſtourdie,
Le mal dont tu deburas mourir.

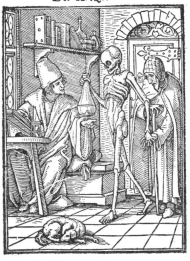

Indica mihi si nosti omnia. Sciebas quod nasciturus
esses, & numerum dierum tuorum noveras?

IOB XXVIII

*Declare if thou knowest it all. Knowest thou it, because
thou wast then born? or because the number of thy
days is great? Job 38:18,21*

Tu dis par Amphibologie
Ce qu'aux aultres doibt advenir.
Dy moy donc par Astrologie
Quand tu deburas a moy venir?

Stulte hac nocte repetunt animam tuam, & quæ par-
asti cuius erunt?

LUCÆ XII

*Thou fool, this night thy soul shall be required of thee:
then whose shall those things be, which thou hast pro-
vided? Luke 12:20*

Ceste nuict la Mort te prendra,
Et demain seras enchassé.
Mais dy moy, fol, a qui viendra
Le bien que tu as amassé?

Der Rych man.

Qui congregat thesauros mendacii vanus & excors
est, & impingetur ad laqueos mortis.
PROVER. XXI

*The getting of treasures by a lying tongue is a vanity tos-
sed to and fro of them that seek death.* Proverbs 21:6

Vain est cil qui amassera
Grandz biens, & tresors pour mentir,
La Mort l'en fera repentir.
Car en ses lacz surpris sera.

Qui volunt divites fieri incidunt in laqueum diaboli,
    & desideria multa, & nociva, quæ mergunt hom⁄
    ines in interitum.

I AD TIMO. VI

But they that will be rich fall into . . . a snare, and into
    many foolish and hurtful lusts, which drown men in
    destruction. I Timothy 6:9

Pour acquerir des biens mondains
Vous entrez en tentation,
Qui vous met es perilz soubdains,
Et vous maine a perdition.

Subito morientur, & in media nocte turbabuntur
populi, & auferent violentum absque manu.

IOB XXXIIII

In a moment shall they die, and the people shall be troub-
led at midnight . . . and the mighty shall be taken
away without hand. Job 34:20

Peuples soubdain s'esleveront
A lencontre de l'inhumain,
Et le violent osteront
D'avec eulx sans force de main.

Der Ritter.

Quoniam cum interierit non sumet secum omnia,
neque cum eo descendet gloria eius.
PSAL. XLVIII

*For when he dieth he shall carry nothing away: his glory
shall not descend after him. Psalm 49:17*

Avec soy rien n'emportera,
Mais qu'une foys la Mort le tombe,
Rien de sa gloire n'ostera,
Pour mettre avec soy en sa tombe.

Der Groff.

Spiritus meus attenuabitur, dies mei breviabuntur, &
solum mihi supereſt sepulchrum.

IOB XVII

My breath is corrupt, my days are extinct, the graves are
ready for me. Job 17:1

Mes esperitz sont attendriz,
Et ma vie s'en va tout beau.
Las mes longz jours sont amoindriz,
Plus ne me reſte qu'un tombeau.

Der Alt man.

Ducunt in bonis dies suos, & in puncto ad inferna
descendunt.

IOB XXI

*They spend their days in wealth, and in a moment go
down to the grave. Job 21:13*

En biens mondains leurs jours despendent
En voluptez, & en tristesse,
Puis soubdain aux Enfers descendent,
Ou leur joye passe en tristesse.

Me & te sola mors separabit.

RUTH I

Death alone shall part me and thee. Ruth 1:17 *

Amour qui unyz nous faict vivre,
En foy noz cueurs preparera,
Qui long temps ne nous pourra suyure,
Car la Mort nous separera.

.

De lectulo super quem ascendisti non descendes, sed
  morte morieris.

IIII REG. I

*Thou shalt not come down from that bed on which thou
  art gone up, but shalt surely die. II Kings 1:4*

Du lict sus lequel as monté
Ne descendras a ton plaisir.
Car Mort t'aura tantost dompté,
Et en brief te viendra saisir.

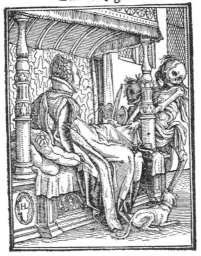

Venite ad me qui onerati estis.

MATTH. XI

Come unto me, all ye that . . . are heavy laden. Mt. 11:28

Venez, & apres moy marchez
Vous qui estes par trop charge.
C'est assez suivy les marchez:
Vous serez par moy decharge.

Der Krämer.

In sudore vultus tui vesceris pane tuo.

GENE. I

In the sweat of thy face shalt thou eat bread. Genesis 3:19

A la sueur de ton visaige
Tu gaigneras ta pauvre vie.
Apres long travail, & usaige,
Voicy la Mort qui te convie.

Der Ackerman.

Homo natus de muliere, brevi vivens tempore re‑
pletur multis miseriis, qui quasi flos egreditur, &
conteritur, & fugit velut umbra.

IOB XIIII

Man that is born of a woman is of few days, and full of
trouble. He cometh forth like a flower, and is cut down:
he fleeth also as a shadow. Job 14:1,2

Tout homme de la femme yssant
Remply de misere, & d'encombre,
Ainsi que fleur tost finissant.
Sort & puis fuyt comme faict l'umbre.

Daß Iung kint.

Omnes ſtabimus ante tribunal domini.

ROMA. XIIII

Vigilate, & orate, quia nescitis qua hora venturus
sit dominus.

MAT. XXIIII

For we shall all stand before the judgment seat of Christ.
Romans 14:10
Watch therefore, and pray: for ye know not what hour
your Lord doth come. Matthew 24:42*

Devant le trosne du grand juge
Chascun de soy compte rendra,
Pourtant veillez, qu'il ne vous juge.
Car ne scavez quand il viendra.

Memorare novissima, & in æternum non peccabis.

ECCLE. VII

Remember the end, and thou shalt never do amiss. Sirach
(*Ecclesiasticus*) 7:36

Si tu veulx vivre sans peché
Voy ceste imaige a tous propos,
Et point ne seras empesché,
Quand tu t'en iras a repos.

& requies æterna,

Melior eſt MORS, quàm uita amara :

quàm languor perſeuerans.

ECCLESIAST. XXX.

Quand le fort armé garde sa court, ce, qu'il possede, est en paix: mais si plus fort que luy survient, il luy oſte toutes ses armures, ausquelles il se conﬁoit.

LUC XI

When a strong man armed keepeth his palace, his goods are in peace: But when a stronger than he shall come upon him, and overcome him, he taketh from him all his armour wherein he trusted. Luke 11:21,22

Le fort armé en jeune corps
Pense avoir seure garnison:
Mais Mort plus forte, le met hors
De sa corporelle maison.

Que profite-il à l'homme, s'il a gaigné tout le Monde,
& qu'il ait perdu son ame?

MATTH. XVI

*For what is a man profited, if he shall gain the whole
world, and lose his own soul? Matthew 16:26*

Que vault à l'homme, tout le Monde
Gaigner d'hazard, & chance experte,
S'il reçoit de sa vie immonde
Par Mort, irreparable perte?

Ne vous enyurez point de vin, auquel eſt dissolution.
EPHES. V

And be not drunk with wine, wherein is excess. Eph. 5:18

De vin (auquel eſt tout exces)
Ne vous enyurez, pour dormir
Sommeil de Mort, qui au deces
Vous face l'ame, & sang vomir.

Comme le bœuf s'en va à la tuerie, & comme le sot
aux ceps pour le chastiement.

PROVERB. VII

As an ox goeth to the slaughter, or as a fool to the correction.
Proverbs 7:22

Le Fol vit en joye, & deduict
Sans sçavoir qu'il s'en va mourant,
Tant qu'à sa fin il est conduict
Ainsi que l'agneau ignorant.

Seigneur, je souffre violentement, guarantis moy.

ISAIE XXXVIII

O Lord, I am oppressed; undertake for me. Isaiah 38:14

La foible femme brigandée
Crie, O seigneur on me fait force.
Lors de Dieu la mort est mandée,
Qui les estrangle à dure estorce.

L'aveugle mene l'aveugle, & tous deux tombent en
la fosse.

MATT. XV

And if the blind lead the blind, both shall fall into the ditch.
Matthew 15:14

L'aveugle un autre aveugle guide,
L'un par l'autre en la fosse tombe:
Car quand plus oultre aller il cuide,
La MORT l'homme jecte en la tombe.

Il cheut en son chariot.
I ROIS IX

He sunk down in his chariot. II Kings 9:24

Au passage de MORT perverse
Raison, Chartier tout esperdu,
Du corps le char, & chevaux verse,
Le vin (sang de vie) espandu.

Moy homme miserable, qui me delivrera de ce corps
subject à la mort?

ROM. VII

O wretched man that I am! who shall deliver me from the
body of this death? Romans 7:24

Qui hors la chair veult en Christ vivre
Ne craint mort, mais dit un mot tel,
Helas, qui me rendra delivre
Pouvre homme de ce corps mortel?

Il sera percé de sagettes.
EXOD. XIX

He shall surely be . . . shot through. Exodus 19:13

L'eage du sens, du sang l'ardeur
Est legier dard, & foible escu
Contre MORT, qui un tel dardeur
De son propre dard rend vaincu.

Les enfans sont trebuchez sur le bois.

THREN. V

The children fell under the wood. Lamentations 5:13

Petiz enfans vont par la voye
Chevauchans baſtons à desrois,
MORT les rue jus: Comme Troye
Perit par ung cheval de bois.

Ceux qui ont leur ventre pour leur Dieu.
PHILIP. III

Whose God is their belly. Philippians 3:19

Comme enfans vivent sans soucy,
Ceux qui font leur dieu de leur ventre
Gros, & gras on les porte: ainsi
MORT les portera secz au centre.

Il partira les despoilles avec les piussans.
ISAIE LIII

He shall divide the spoil with the strong. Isaiah 53:12

Pour les victoires triumphées
Sur les plus forts des humains cœurs,
Les despoilles dresse en trophées
La MORT vaincresse des vainqueurs.

Sois fidele jusques à la mort: & je te donneray la coronne de vie. Qui vaincra, il n'aura point de nuisance de la mort seconde.

APOC. II

Be thou faithful unto death, and I will give thee a crown of life. He that overcometh shall not be hurt of the second death. Revelation 2:10,11

Qui triomphent en leurs delices,
Ont l'horrible Mort qui les suit:
Mais vertu à vie conduit
Ceux qui auront dompté les vices.

De la femme est le commencement de peché, & par
elle mourrons tous.

ECCLESIAST. XXV

*Of the woman came the beginning of sin, and through her
we all die. Sirach (Ecclesiasticus) 25:24*

Par Eve estant d'Adam l'espouse
Nasquit peché, d'ou vint la Mort.
Espouse donc ne te courrouce
Si, comme tous, la Mort te mord.

Quelle chose defraude la vie? la Mort.
ECCLESIAST. XXXI
Aie donc souvenance que la mort ne tarde point.
ECCLE. IX

What taketh away life? Death. Sirach (Ecclesiasticus)
31:34 (Douay version)
Remember that wrath will not tarry long. Sirach (Eccle-
siasticus) 7:16

Espoux, la Mort est ennemie
De nostre vie & la poursuit:
Voy donc qu'au plus beau de ta vie
A ta fin elle te conduit.

L'homme n'a puissance du jour de la Mort: & n'a delivrance en guerre: & la malice ne delivrera pas son maiſtre.

ECCLESIASTE VIII

There is no man that hath power . . . in the day of death: and there is no discharge in that war; neither shall wickedness deliver those that are given to it. Ecclesiastes 8:8

L'homme avec toute sa puissance
Ne pourra la Mort eschapper,
Qui tout soudain le vient happer
Lors qu'il poursuit sa delivrance.

Ils ont longuement erré en la voie d'erreur eſtans
deceuz en maniere d'enfans, pour ce leur as⸝tu
donné jugement à derision, comme à enfans sans
raison.

SAP. XII

*For they went astray very far in the ways of error, . . .
being deceived, as children of no understanding. Therefore unto them, as to children without the use of reason, thou didst send a judgment to mock them. Wisdom of Solomon 12:24,25*

Qui du tout suivent leurs desirs,
Sont comme enfans sans jugement:
Et au milieu de leurs plaisirs
La Mort les conduit au torment.

This book was conceived and designed by Katharine
Homans and Amy Montague who have printed it to-
gether. The presswork is by Katharine Homans; the
text was edited by Amy Montague. The type, Bembo
and Poliphilus, was set by Michael & Winifred Bixler.
The photoengravings were made by The Mohawk
Engraving Company. The 950 copies of the trade
edition, of which 100 are for the members of the
Cygnet Press, were bound by Robert Burlen
& Son. Arno Werner bound by hand the
seventy copies of the deluxe edition.
The books were completed on
September third, 1974.

THE CYGNET PRESS
Philip Hofer
Katharine Homans
Amy Montague